Editor **Andrea Woof**

Photo Illustrator **John Chew-land**

Writer **Hairy Growling**

Designer **Beth Beagler**

Photo Editors **Marguerite Schropp Poocharelli, Annmarie Arfvila**

Copy Editor **Megan Collies**

Reporter **Jeremy Repan-fetch**

SI Premedia **Geoffrey Mutt-chaud, Dan Barkin,
Ge-retriever Burke, Sandra Valle-hound**

Managing Editor, SPORTS ILLUSTRATED KIDS **Bob Grr**

For my pack... Thank you for your patience and
the occasional scratch behind the ear.
— *John Ueland*

HOME ENTERTAINMENT

TIME HOME ENTERTAINMENT
Publisher: Jim Childs
Vice President, Brand & Digital Strategy: Steven Sandonato
Executive Director, Marketing Services: Carol Pittard
Executive Director, Retail & Special Sales: Tom Mifsud
Executive Publishing Director: Joy Butts
Director, Bookazine Development & Marketing: Laura Adam
Finance Director: Glenn Buonocore
Associate Publishing Director: Megan Pearlman
Assistant General Counsel: Helen Wan
Assistant Director, Special Sales: Ilene Schreider
Senior Book Production Manager: Susan Chodakiewicz
Design & Prepress Manager: Anne-Michelle Gallero
Brand Manager: Jonathan White
Associate Prepress Manager: Alex Voznesenskiy
Assistant Brand Manager: Stephanie Braga

Editorial Director: Stephen Koepp

Special thanks: Katherine Barnet, Jeremy Biloon, Rose Cirrincione,
Jacqueline Fitzgerald, Christine Font, Jenna Goldberg, Hillary Hirsch,
David Kahn, Amy Mangus, Kimberly Marshall, Amy Migliaccio, Nina
Mistry, Dave Rozzelle, Ricardo Santiago, Adriana Tierno, Vanessa Wu

ISBN 10: 1-61893-051-6
ISBN 13: 978-1-61893-051-4
Library of Congress Control Number: 2013935572
SPORTS ILLUSTRATED KIDS is a trademark of Time Inc.

We welcome your comments and suggestions about
SPORTS ILLUSTRATED KIDS Books.
Please write to us at:
SPORTS ILLUSTRATED KIDS Books
Attention: Book Editors
P.O. Box 11016
Des Moines, IA 50336-1016

If you would like to order any of our hardcover Collector's Edition
books, please call us at 1-800-327-6388 (Monday through Friday,
7 a.m. to 8 p.m., or Saturday, 7 a.m. to 6 p.m., Central Time).

1 QGV 13

TOP DOGS

Sports Illustrated KIDS

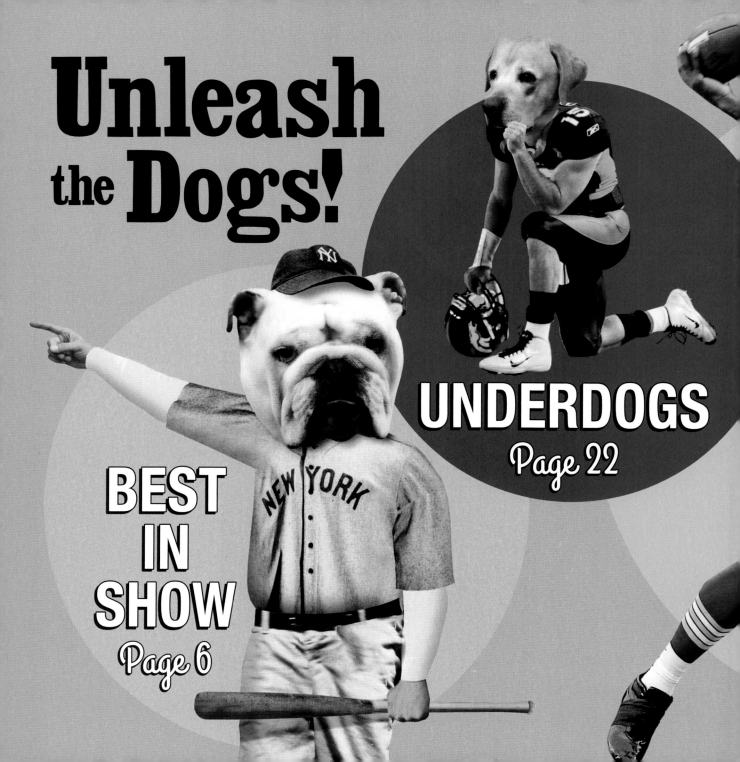

Unleash the Dogs!

UNDERDOGS
Page 22

BEST IN SHOW
Page 6

MOST
VALUABLE
PUPPIES
Page 40

EVERY DOG
HAS ITS DAY
Page 30

HOT
DOGS
Page 52

The Great Air Jor-Dane

The Great Air Jor-Dane and Sir Charles Bark-ley —
also known as the Round Hound of Rebound — were
two of the greatest when it came to jumping through
hoops. But they were often fighting over the same
bone, so teaming up was a new trick for these old
dogs. They learned to play nice together and made a
great team, leading the U.S. to a first-place medal for
bassetball at the 1992 Olympics.

Babe Ruff

Babe Ruff marked his territory among baseball's legends with one mighty swing in Game 3 of the 1932 World Series. Stepping out of the batter's box, the New Yorkie Yankee pointed to the centerfield bleachers. Some say he was predicting a home run. Others think he merely spotted a squirrel in the stands. Either way, the kennel went wild when Ruff blasted a home run on the very next pitch.

Tennis GrrrEats!

Ruffa Nadal  Rover Federer

Ruffa Nadal		Rover Federer
6' 1"	**Height (on hind legs)**	6' 1"
3 years, 10 months (27 in human years)	**Age**	4 years, 7 months (32 in human years)
8 French Bulldog Open titles	**Greatest Accomplishment**	7 Wimbledog titles
Bark-spin shot	**Biggest Strength**	Baseline fore-paw
Gets so excited that he can't sit and stay	**Biggest Weakness**	Always falls for old "throw a fake tennis ball" trick
Kibbles	**Favorite Treat**	Bits

The All-Time Best Musher

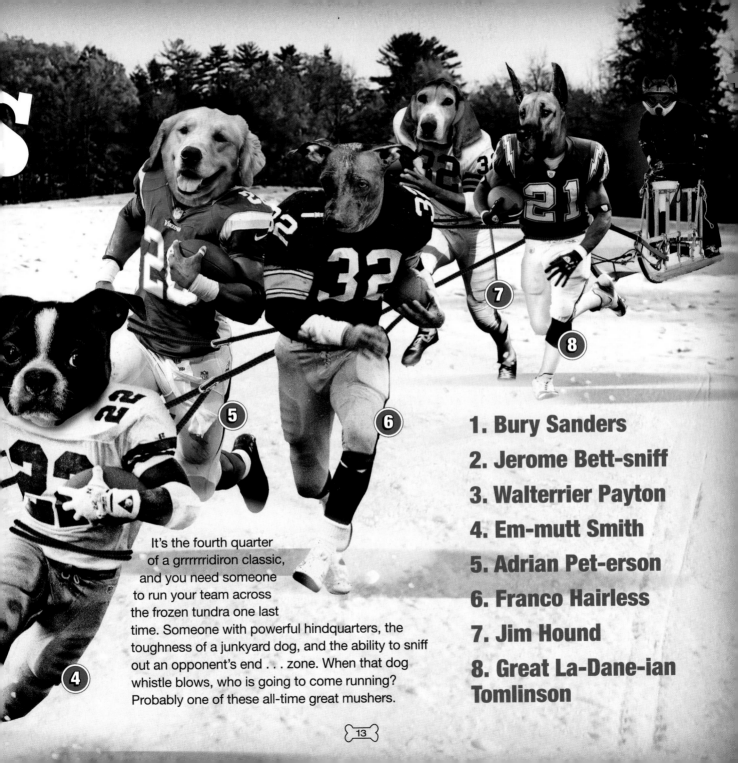

It's the fourth quarter of a grrrrrridiron classic, and you need someone to run your team across the frozen tundra one last time. Someone with powerful hindquarters, the toughness of a junkyard dog, and the ability to sniff out an opponent's end . . . zone. When that dog whistle blows, who is going to come running? Probably one of these all-time great mushers.

1. Bury Sanders
2. Jerome Bett-sniff
3. Walterrier Payton
4. Em-mutt Smith
5. Adrian Pet-erson
6. Franco Hairless
7. Jim Hound
8. Great La-Dane-ian Tomlinson

These Dogs Know What to Do With a Stick!

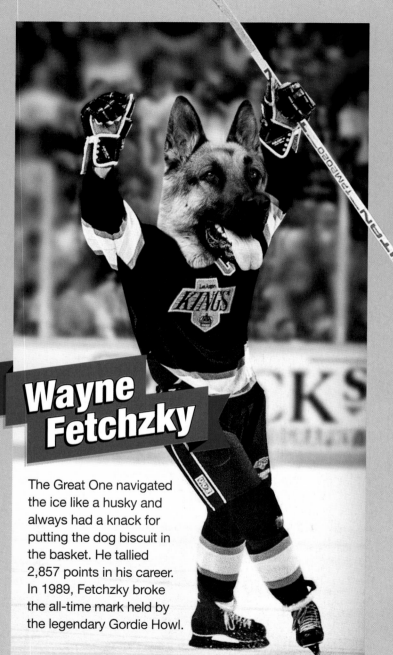

Wayne Fetchzky

The Great One navigated the ice like a husky and always had a knack for putting the dog biscuit in the basket. He tallied 2,857 points in his career. In 1989, Fetchzky broke the all-time mark held by the legendary Gordie Howl.

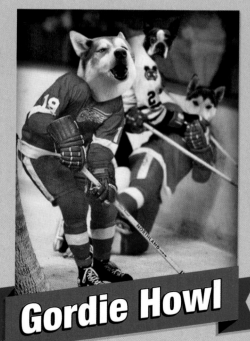

Gordie Howl

Arnold Palmeranian

Before there was Tiger Woofs, or even Jack Nicklassie, Arnold Palmeranian ruled the Kennel Club. No one could send a drive down a dogleg like Palmeranian. And could this mutt ever putt. He won the Masters (a tournament run by dog owners) four times. He became such an icon that his signature drink — iced tea mixed with lemonade mixed with toilet water — became a popular thirst-quencher for dogs everywhere.

All-Star Relievers

Sure, a dalmatian might be able to help put out a fire. But if you need to escape a hot situation, you want one of these puppies by the fire hydrant. Mariano Ruff-vera and Billy Wagger were stars in New Yorkie; Collie Fingers did his business for the Oakland Athle-ticks; and Trevor Ruffman set records with the San Diego Pet-dres. All four marked their territory in the ninth inning.

1. Mariano Ruff-vera
2. Billy Wagger
3. Collie Fingers
4. Trevor Ruffman

Michael Stray-han

Michael Stray-han buried quarterbacks like most dogs bury bones. He holds the single-season record of 22½ sacks. Along with teammates Heel-i Manning and Osi Umenyorkie, he helped the G-Dogs win the Lom-barky Trophy as Super Bowl XLII champs.

Pooches Ruff

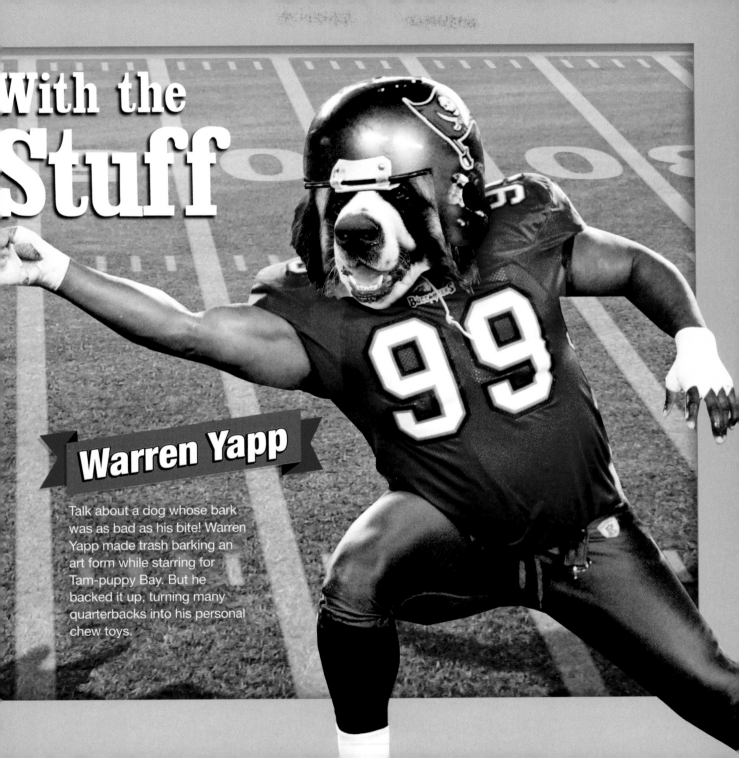

With the
Stuff

Warren Yapp

Talk about a dog whose bark was as bad as his bite! Warren Yapp made trash barking an art form while starring for Tam-puppy Bay. But he backed it up, turning many quarterbacks into his personal chew toys.

HONUS
WAGGER

ICHIRO
SHIH TZUKI

WADE
DOGGS

DOG
HALL OF
FAME

These alpha dogs separated
themselves from the pack

**PUG
RODRIGUEZ**

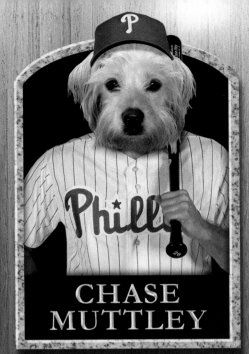

**CHASE
MUTTLEY**

**PAWS
MOLITOR**

**ALBERT
POODLES**

Mini Mutts

Bark Twain once said, "It's not the size of the dog in the fight, it's the size of the fight in the dog." And that's especially true of these pint-sized pups. They may look like runts of the litter, but each of these scrappers have become big dogs in their sports. Lionel Muttsi is the world's best in soc-grr (or, as they call it in most countries, pawball). Dustin Pet-droia earned his "dirt dog" nickname with his gritty play and refusal to take baths. Wes Welkarf is a fetching machine, while Maurice Jones-Drool has spent years mushing through opposing packs. And while bassetball is usually a sport for big dogs, little guys like Puggsy Bogues and Nate Slobberson became successes on the houndcourt.

Dustin Pet-droia

So cute you just want to **pinscher** them!

Tim Te-Bow-Wow
A Quarterbark's Tail

THE DRAFT
How much is that doggie in the window? Enough that Den-grrrr traded for an extra first-round pick in order to take him home.

April 2010

December 2007

HEISDOG TROPHY WINNER
Te-Bow-Wow first became a star at obedience school. The leader and quarterbark for the University of Floridog, he captured a major award in 2007 when he won the Heisdog Trophy.

January 2012

YOU GOTTA BELIEVE!
Not everyone thought Te-Bow-Wow could play. Sure, he had powerful hind legs and was a natural alpha dog — when he barked, other dogs listened. But there were questions about his throwing paw. Still, he got a chance to start for Den-grrr late in the 2011 season, and boy did it pick the right dog. Te-Bow-Wow led the team to six straight wins, and on January 8 took it to a playoff win over Muttsburgh.

TE-BOW-WOWING

Te-Bow-Wow was winning games, and his personality was winning over fans. Te-Bow-Wowing became the hottest new trend, as dogs everywhere took a knee and bowed their snout into a clenched paw. But the amazing run in Den-grrr ended suddenly. Living legend Panting Manning was released by Indian-alpo-lis. Den-grrr signed him, and Te-Bow-Wow was traded to New Yorkie.

January 2012

THE FUTURE?

What does the future hold for Te-Bow-Wow? No one knows for sure. But Chew England signed him to a contract, and he'll have a chance to run around behind legendary quarterbark Pom Brady. Maybe it will work out for Te-Bow-Wow, maybe it won't. But one thing is for sure: This pup has the dogged determination to work his tail off no matter what.

September 2012

BACK ON THE LEASH

Te-Bow-Wow's one season in New Yorkie was a disaster. The team struggled with Bark Sanchez running the offense. But still, Te-Bow-Wow stayed on his leash, moping on the sidelines. He could only watch as this group of bad dogs won only six games.

BUSTER DOGLEASH
KOs Champ
★ ★ ★
BITE TYSON

Buster Dogleash was the ultimate underdog. The young boxer was thrown to the wolves when he faced Bite Tyson, one of the most dominant and fearsome boxers of all time. But Dogleash was tough, and he hung in against the champ. With Tyson panting with exhaustion, Dogleash landed a combination of punches to the champ's snout, knocking him down for the count. It was the biggest shock since the invention of the invisible dog fence. And with the win, Dogleash captured the heavyweight collar.

Pug Flutie

In pawball, quarterbarks are usually taller dogs – Great Danes, German shepherds – not pugs like Flutie. But when this dog had the ball, even the best dog catchers couldn't get ahold of him. Flutie's ultimate highlight was when he led his Paws-ton College Beagles to a stunning win over the Miami Hairy-canes. With the Beagles trailing 45–41 in the final seconds, it might have looked as if he was chasing his tail on the final play. But really he was just running circles around would-be tacklers. Once he found an opening, he launched a pass as far as he could. The Hairy-cane defenders misjudged Flutie's paw strength, and the ball sailed like a Frisbee over the defense and into the paws of a Beagles retriever.

Paws-itively Amazing!

Now THAT'S

Something to Howl About!

Sir Rover Bannister

For Rover Bannister, there was no such thing as going for a walk. This dog only ran, and he ran so fast that in 1954 he became the first to achieve a four-minute mile. He was a hero in his home country, as Yorkies, English bulldogs, and Scottish terriers across Greyhound Britain celebrated his accomplishment over tea and dog biscuits. Twenty-one years later, he became Sir Rover Bannister. Because of his four-minute feat on four feet, he was knighted by Queen Eliza-fetch II.

Landon Doberman

It was desperation time for Team USA in the 2010 World Bowl. Needing a late goal, star midfielder Landon Doberman led these underdogs back into contention. He chased down a loose ball and put it in the net to give the U.S. the goal they needed to advance in the tournament.

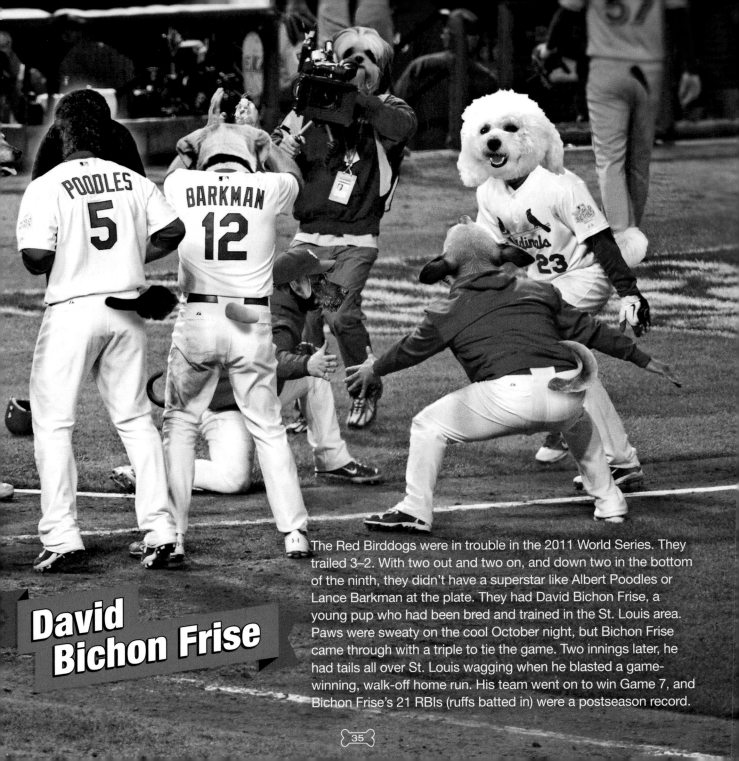

David Bichon Frise

The Red Birddogs were in trouble in the 2011 World Series. They trailed 3–2. With two out and two on, and down two in the bottom of the ninth, they didn't have a superstar like Albert Poodles or Lance Barkman at the plate. They had David Bichon Frise, a young pup who had been bred and trained in the St. Louis area. Paws were sweaty on the cool October night, but Bichon Frise came through with a triple to tie the game. Two innings later, he had tails all over St. Louis wagging when he blasted a game-winning, walk-off home run. His team went on to win Game 7, and Bichon Frise's 21 RBIs (ruffs batted in) were a postseason record.

Slobber Griffin III is one of those dogs who will run around the lawn all day. And none of the other dogs can catch him. The star quarterbark howls out the plays, takes the ball, and then leaves behind a trail of would-be tacklers (and drool). And this dog can throw the ball, too. Nothing baffles opponents more than the play he's always itching to run: the flea flicker.

When in Doubt, Go With a Flea Flicker

Greatest Fetc

Jim Shed-monds

An-drool Jones

ners

These rovers loved chasing down balls at the dog park. They were the best at bringing in the tough catches. In the 1954 World Series, Will-leash Mays made a grab so amazing that it's known simply as "The Fetch." Kirby Pug-ett made highlight reel after highlight reel with his catches at Minnesota's Pet-rodome. You could be sure that An-drool Jones was going to come back clutching the ball — even if it was always covered in slobber. And Jim Shed-monds could always be counted on to make acrobatic doggie dives.

Kirby Pug-ett

Will-leash Mays

Some Excellent

Heel-i Manning

Panting Manning

Breeds

Some dogs are simply bred for greatness. That's the case with Arfie Manning and his litter of puppies, which included Panting and Heel-i Manning. The Manning pups were born to be quarterbarks. So even though Arfie used to get his tail kicked while playing with a bunch of bad dogs in Chew Orleans, Panting (playing for Indian-alpo-lis and Den-grr) and Heel-i (the New Yorkie QB) have become champions.

Arfie Manning

Like father, like pup. Ken Gruffey Jr. was famous for chasing down balls all over the yard, just like his dad used to do.

Doc was a tough guard dog who now leads his own pack. His son, Austin, is still a young pup who has shown promise while getting house-trained in Chew Orleans.

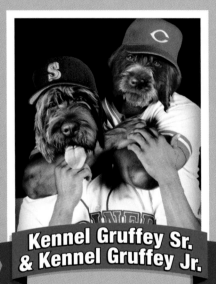

Kennel Gruffey Sr. & Kennel Gruffey Jr.

Doc & Austin Rovers

Chipper Bones

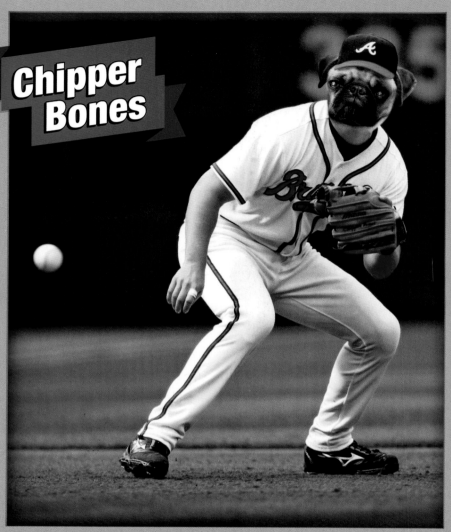

It's not always easy for a young pup to play with the big dogs. But that's exactly what Chipper Bones did. He made his big-league debut when he was 3 years old (21 in human years), and even though a paw injury limited him early in his career, he quickly grew into a legend for the Arflanta Braves. With his ability to bat the ball around with his right and left paw, he won Most Valuable Puppy in 1999.

Big Puppy

For a while, he was the puppy that no one wanted. He lived with a team in Minnesota, but eventually it decided to send him away. Big Puppy waited at the pet store every day, until finally a nice team from Paws-ton brought him home to Fur-nway Park. In his new yard, Big Puppy won over fans with his long home runs and his big smile. He helped Paws-ton break the Curse of the Bam-beagle in 2004, and in 2007 they won the big one in October again.

Friends Fur-ever

Sidney Cros-beagle

and

Arf-geni Malkin

The fortunes of the Muttsburgh Penguins started to change when the team added a couple of purebred stars. Because of his talent, Sidney Cros-beagle grew up in the spotlight, being coached by top dog trainers and getting to eat plenty of people food. Cros-beagle has become a pack leader, taking the Penguins to the Stan-leash Cup title in 2009. But he couldn't have done it without Arf-geni Malkin, who grew up playing against Siberian huskies in Russia. While he had to adjust to being the new dog in Cros-beagle's house, Malkin ended up becoming a top dog himself when he won the Most Valuable Puppy award in 2012.

This Pup Can SWIM!
(And Not Just Doggie Paddle)

Michael Yelps

Bark Spitz won seven gold dog tags at the 1972 Olympics, a record that seemed unbreakable. But then Michael Yelps brought his doggie paddle to the Pekingese Games. Yelps swam so fast that some onlookers thought he was actually a seal. While competitors were lapping up water, Yelps was lapping them. By the time he was done shaking the water off his coat, he had a record eight gold dog tags, a mark that isn't within barking distance.

The Tail of

Cavalier King James

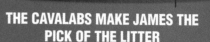

THE CHOSEN ONE

Maybe it was his talent, or his drive, or maybe it was simply because he was the only puppy who insisted on wearing a headband. But while he was still in obedience school, King James was already a star. So much so that, while he was still a pup, he appeared on the cover of *Pooch Illustrated*.

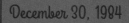

December 30, 1984

February 18, 2002

June 26, 2003

CAVALIER KING JAMES IS BORN

It was a happy day at Akron Veterinary Hospital, when King James was born. Early on, it was clear that King James was different from his fellow puppies. When most dogs play fetch, they get the ball and bring it back to their master. King James would get the ball, knock over other dogs on the way back, then ram it through a hoop.

Pooch Illustrated

Winter Olympics
WHAT MAKES THESE
GAMES SO SPECIAL
U.S. SNOWBOARDERS
...E THE HALFPIPE

THE CHOSEN ONE

High school junior
Cavalier King James
would be an NBA
lottery pick right now

THE CAVALABS MAKE JAMES THE PICK OF THE LITTER

The day had come for King James to head out into the world. Teams from around the National Bassetball Association were lined up to pick their favorite puppies to bring home. The Cavalabs chose first and made King James the pick of the litter. While he was a star for his team, King James could never quite bring home the bacon for the Cavalabs.

CHAMPIONS

Success didn't come immediately, and there were plenty of dog days early on for this newly formed pack. Like pups who get to the beach only to see a big No Dogs Allowed sign, they made it all the way to the Finals only to lose to the Dalmatian Mavericks. The next year was different, though. King James took his teammates back to the Finals, and these dogs were not afraid of the Thunder, which they beat in five games. King James finally got his first bassetball title.

June 21, 2012

July 8, 2010

CAVALIER KING JAMES SPANIEL ANNOUNCES "THE DECISION" WITH JIM GREYHOUND

In July 2010, the world waited as Cavalier King James got ready to announce whether or not he'd don a shiny new coat the following season. In an interview with Jim Greyhound, James barked that he would leave Cleveland and take his talents (the ability to leap on command) to South Beach. Since then, he's been in Cleveland's doghouse.

October 2010

BRING IT

Along with Dwyane Wag and Chris Lab-Bosh-Dor, King James combined to form the most amazing dog team since Scooby-Doo and Dynomutt.

Well-Groomed

David Bark-ham was as famous for being a handsome show dog as he was for his soccer ball tricks. Troy Poodle-malu's shiny coat landed him spots in shampoo commercials (for Head & Shoulders Flea & Tick Control). Bichon White's stylish aerial maneuvers put Air Bud to shame. And the always flamboyant Perro Martinez helped take down baseball's famous Curse of the Bam-beagle. The way they strut, these are the kinds of dogs you'd be proud to take on a walk … just make sure you bring a plastic bag for cleanup.

Perro Martinez

David Bark-ham

STANDARD POODLE

STANDARD POODLE

Bichon
White

Troy
Poodle-malu

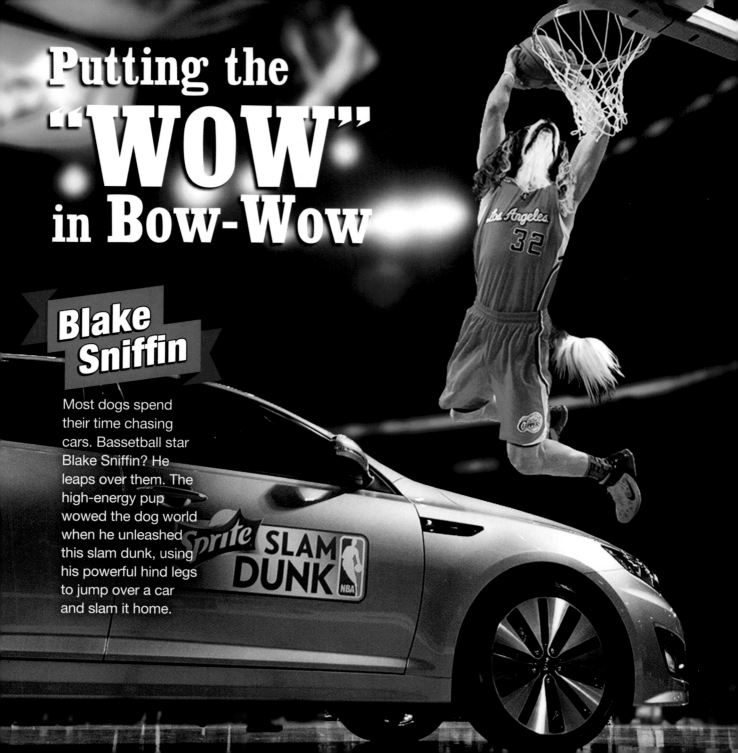

Putting the "WOW" in Bow-Wow

Blake Sniffin

Most dogs spend their time chasing cars. Bassetball star Blake Sniffin? He leaps over them. The high-energy pup wowed the dog world when he unleashed this slam dunk, using his powerful hind legs to jump over a car and slam it home.

Snarl Edwards

You don't need to give this dog a treat to see a trick. Snarl Edwards does flips after his victories. Driving in traditional dog fashion — head out the window and tongue wagging — Edwards has more than 60 career wins.

Want to see a pack of wild dogs? Just watch what happens when Green Bay takes one to the doghouse. Any time one of the Pack-arfs, like wide retriever Donald Drive-grrr, scores a touchdown, he celebrates with the signature Lam-bone Leap. The fans of the green and Old Yeller . . . er, yellow, can't help howling over being close enough to give their heroes congratulatory pats and tummy rubs.

The Lam-bone Leap

TOP DOGS
Dogs Are People Too

Best in Show

The Great Air Jor-Dane   **Michael Jordan**
Basketball

Charles Bark-ley   **Charles Barkley**
Basketball

Babe Ruff   Babe Ruth
Baseball

Ruffa Nadal   **Rafael Nadal**
Tennis

Rover Federer   **Roger Federer**
Tennis

Bury Sanders   **Barry Sanders**
Football

Jerome Bett-sniff   **Jerome Bettis**
Football

Walterrier Payton   **Walter Payton**
Football

Em-mutt Smith   **Emmitt Smith**
Football

Adrian Pet-erson   **Adrian Peterson**
Football

Franco Hairless   **Franco Harris**
Football

Jim Hound | **Jim Brown**

Football

Great La-Dane-ian Tomlinson | **LaDainian Tomlinson**

Football

Wayne Fetchzky | **Wayne Gretzky**

Hockey

Gordie Howl | **Gordie Howe**

Hockey

Arnold Palmeranian | **Arnold Palmer**

Golf

Mariano Ruff-vera | **Mariano Rivera**

Baseball

Billy Wagger | **Billy Wagner**

Baseball

Collie Fingers | **Rollie Fingers**

Baseball

Trevor Ruffman | **Trevor Hoffman**

Baseball

Michael Stray-han | **Michael Strahan**

Football

Warren Yapp | **Warren Sapp**

Football

Honus Wagger | **Honus Wagner**

Baseball

Wade Doggs | **Wade Boggs**

Baseball

Ichiro Shih Tzuki | **Ichiro Suzuki**

Baseball

Pug Rodriguez | **Iván (Pudge) Rodriguez**

Baseball

Paws Molitor | **Paul Molitor**

Baseball

Chase Muttley | **Chase Utley**

Baseball

Albert Poodles | **Albert Pujols**

Baseball

Dustin Pet-droia | **Dustin Pedroia**

Baseball

Maurice Jones-Drool | **Maurice Jones-Drew**

Football

Lionel Muttsi | **Lionel Messi**

Soccer

Puggsy Bogues | **Muggsy Bogues**

Basketball

Wes Welkarf | **Wes Welker**

Football

Nate Slobberson | **Nate Robinson**

Basketball

Tim Te-Bow-Wow | **Tim Tebow**

Football

Buster Dogleash | **Buster Douglas**

Boxing

Bite Tyson | **Mike Tyson**

Boxing

Pug Flutie | **Doug Flutie**

Football

Sir Rover Bannister | **Sir Roger Bannister**

Track and Field

Landon Doberman | **Landon Donovan**

Soccer

David Bichon Frise | **David Freese**

Baseball

Slobber Griffin III | **Robert Griffin III**

Football

Jim Shed-monds | **Jim Edmonds**

Baseball

An-drool Jones | **Andruw Jones**

Baseball

Will-leash Mays | **Willie Mays**

Baseball

 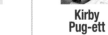

Kirby Pug-ett | **Kirby Puckett**

Baseball

EVERY DOG Has Its Day

MVPs — MOST VALUABLE PUPPIES

Heel-i Manning | **Eli Manning**

Football

Panting Manning **Peyton Manning**
Football

Arfie Manning **Archie Manning**
Football

Kennel Gruffey Sr. **Ken Griffey Sr.**
Baseball

Kennel Gruffey Jr. **Ken Griffey Jr.**
Baseball

Doc Rovers **Doc Rivers**
Basketball

Austin Rovers **Austin Rivers**
Basketball

Chipper Bones **Chipper Jones**
Baseball

Big Puppy **David (Big Papi) Ortiz**
Baseball

Sidney Cros-beagle **Sidney Crosby**
Hockey

Arf-geni Malkin **Evgeni Malkin**
Hockey

Michael Yelps **Michael Phelps**
Swimming

Cavalier King James **LeBron James**
Basketball

Perro Martinez **Pedro Martinez**
Baseball

David Bark-ham **David Beckham**
Soccer

Bichon White **Shaun White**
Snowboarding

Troy Poodle-malu **Troy Polamalu**
Football

Blake Sniffin **Blake Griffin**
Basketball

Snarl Edwards **Carl Edwards**
Auto Racing

Donald Drive-grr **Donald Driver**
Football